Lung Capacity

Lung Capacity

Lung Capacity

Copyright © 2024 by Mae Setrova

All rights reserved

No portion of this book may be reproduced in any form without written permission from the author, except as permitted by U.S. copyright law.

Instagram: @maesetrovapoet
TikTok: @maesetrovapoet
Email: maeswrites337@gmail.com

Lung Capacity

Lung Capacity

Author's Note

Nearly every poem in this book is 2-3 years old. They're pieces I wrote when I first began sharing my work online for the world to see and for a few months while writing this, I thought about scratching this idea as a whole and focusing on a different book, one with all my current work in it that speaks more about who I am rather than who I was but these poems have healed and helped thousands of people, myself included. So while they are older, they are still true and they are evidence of my own growth, struggles and things I have overcome despite everything. Who I am today wouldn't exist if it wasn't for the version of me who wrote these poems as a way to cope. I wouldn't have gotten through the things I did or have the opportunities that I do without them, so they deserve to be the first I publish and share in this way.

Lung Capacity

Lung Capacity

Content Warning:

*Suicidal Urges & Attempts
Brief mention of Domestic Violence
Grief & Death
Emotional Abuse*

please contact a suicide hotline if you are considering ending your life or harming yourself. reach out for help from family or friends (if possible) when these urges increase.

Lung Capacity

Lung Capacity

TABLE OF CONTENTS

Title	0
Copyright	2
Author's Note	4
Content Warning.	6
Table of Contents	8
Dedication	10
Playlist.	12
For My Mother & Father	14
For the Heart That Still Bleeds	50
For the Wounded Minds	134
For the Souls That Ache	166
Endnote	175
About Author	178

Lung Capacity

Lung Capacity

*For anyone who clings to the what-ifs and grieves
what will never be.*

Lung Capacity

Lung Capacity

PLAYLISTS

spotify

apple music

Lung Capacity

Lung Capacity

For my mother & father
complex parental relationships, motherhood.

Lung Capacity

My father.

A man who managed to be physically present but emotionally absent for the majority of my life. We lived under the same roof and still managed to keep missing each other entirely. I avoided him at times when he was home and he never thought to seek me out. Displaying affection and saying things like *"I love you"* never was his strong suit but it was never mine either so I guess he's not the only one at fault for the state of our relationship. I'm told I should be grateful I had him there at all but what good does it do to have somebody if they are never really there in the way that counts? I love him because he's my father but I do not know him the way a child should know the man that makes up half of them.

I can only give you the title of who he is to me and nothing about who he really is.

Lung Capacity

"Is anger always this loud?"
I asked my father while we sat around a fire.

"No," he said,
*"Sometimes it doesn't even make a sound
and that is the worst kind of anger"*

Lung Capacity

I wonder who my father would be today if his childhood had been different. Maybe he could have learned to love a little bit better, less afraid of it because it wouldn't be so unfamiliar to him if instead of the abuse he endured, he was truly loved. Raised by soft hands and gentle words — a mother who read him stories and a father who felt pride looking at his boy. Maybe that would have made a difference in the way he expressed himself. The rage humming on the edge of his fingertips never would have been born and in its place, there would be a calmness to him. One he always deserved to feel but was never allowed. Who would my father be today if such an emotion was easy to identify and express?

Lung Capacity

I'm more my father than I am my mother. I'm concentration angered when interrupted and laughter that takes effort to hear. I love quietly but drastically — I would sever my arm off and hand it over to someone in need and I wouldn't dare to think twice about the consequences until I'm faced with them but I stumble over the words *"I love you"* like small children do over pebbles.

I was born and my mother gave me her smile but the heart I call mine beats rhythmically with my father's. It's as if he pulled his own out of his chest and placed it in mine to ensure he would always find some piece of himself within me because he knew I would grow to look so much like her and so little like him. My mom gave birth to me but I have a feeling that I was crafted from the same fabrics my dad was, and I do not say it often but I take pride in being even the slightest bit like him. *Concentration angered when interrupted and laughter that takes effort to hear.*

Lung Capacity

Two scratch-off tickets and a quarter found beneath a pack of cigarettes in the cup holders. A monster can placed next to a blue bug juice and the sound of the gas pump clicking off. Summer breeze fills the entire car while my dad and I have our arms placed on the center console scratching our tickets off one at a time, passing the quarter back and forth until all the numbers are revealed.

We never won more than $20 on a scratch-off during that time but we did laugh, and even our losses felt like victories when we shared a bag of beef jerky on the way home and spoke of the wonders of the world.

Lung Capacity

I'm watching a movie while eating my dinner alone and I remember all the times my father would come home after a long day of work and ask me if I wanted to watch a movie with him and I said no. I was busy doing what teenage girls do and with each rejection I handed out to him the less he asked until eventually he never asked me again. I picture my father sitting in his chair like I am right now, watching a movie and eating his dinner alone while the rest of the house slept or had company to keep and my heart begins to feel like it's breaking.

When my father comes home I ask him if he wants to watch a movie with me. I watch his face light up like a child's on Christmas morning and I put his favorite film on. We eat our dinner together and discuss the day's events and laugh at the same scenes. He tells me bad jokes while making us popcorn and as he adds salt & pepper to the bowl, I begin to feel like a little kid again.

Lung Capacity

At six years old I used to run to the front door of my childhood home to greet my dad when he came home. I distinctly remember the sounds of his vehicle pulling into the driveway sending volts of excitement through me and dropping everything I was doing at that moment to race my sister to the front door to welcome him home with hugs formed by tiny arms and the magic of children's laughter. I sometimes wonder if he remembers these things too. If he would wait on the other side of the door listening to my sister and I giggle, waiting for the perfect moment to open the door to two little girls wearing wide grins yelling *"Daddy!"*. I wonder if he ever misses that the way I do, if he finds himself waiting on the other side of the door sometimes before remembering we are no longer little girls waiting for his return. *I wonder if he cries when he remembers it the way I do.*

Lung Capacity

As a child, the toys I favored were always the ones my dad brought home for me after days or weeks away. From the big yellow dog I got at 3 and the tiny stuffed buffalo he got while down in Colorado, I always gave them a little extra care than the rest. They were evidence that while he was away and drowning in work, he still thought of me. I do not think this was my father trying to buy my love as a kid or an attempt to erase the fact he was gone so much, but rather his way of saying our love for each other didn't falter just because of the distance put between us.

Lung Capacity

In another world, my mother does not become a mother. She doesn't meet my dad or at the very least, she never falls in love with him. Instead, she goes on to attend a college out of state and pursues all of her dreams. She travels the world in her free time, taking photos in France and trying new foods in Tokyo and maybe she adopts a dog, a four-year-old golden retriever who sees the world with her and she never has to wonder about *what ifs* in life because she is too busy living it to ever second guess her life choices or wonder what she is missing.

In another world, I do not exist.
But my mother gets to *live*, not just *survive*.

Lung Capacity

My mother will not see me grow old.

She will not see my skin wrinkle
or my hair begin to wilt.
She won't meet my grandchildren,
or see what becomes of me when I'm 80.
She is the creator of my life
but still only a small moment of it.

She has held my hand and watched
as my body took its very first breath
but she won't be there to hold it as I take my final.

My mother is my entire life,
and still merely passing through it.

Lung Capacity

She's my mother. Of course she has hurt me.
Of course she has caused damage that can't be undone
or fixed or maybe even forgiven.
She's my mother, but she is still human.

I see her best and worst qualities
side by side when I look at her.
She is both the woman I hope to someday be
and the woman I pray I'll never become.

Mae Setrova

Lung Capacity

Your body has never been yours, has it? It was your mothers, then my fathers and then it was ours —— your womb the first home to three children and a land full of scars gathered from it. It has always belonged to somebody else in some form of a way and I think because of this, you have never learned how to care for it unless it was for another individual.

You have never cared for yourself, mama.
And you wonder where I learned to do the same.

Lung Capacity

I'm 7 and growing pains mean my legs hurt after a long day spent playing outside and I need my mother to rub them until I fall asleep.

I'm 12 and growing pains mean I just started my first period and I need my mother to place a heating pad on my lower stomach and tell me what this means.

I'm 16 and growing pains mean my first boyfriend broke my heart for the first time and I need my mother to hold the pieces of what's left together.

I'm 23 and growing pains mean my father just called me to say we have to put my childhood dog down and I need my mother's shoulder to cry on as I say goodbye.

I'm 27 and growing pains mean I have just given birth and I need my mother to tell me how to do this because I am scared.

I'm 68 and the growing pains continue to come. They only mean different things at different ages but I always need my mother.

Mae Setrova

Lung Capacity

My mother wasn't always a mother. She wasn't always a married woman with children and a house she'd spend the day caring for. Sometimes that slips my mind. Sometimes I forget my mother was once just a child, a little girl in a dress playing with Barbies and stuffed toys while a pair of muddy rain boots rested next to the front door. I forget that at one point, she and my father were strangers and she was just a teenage girl admiring a boy from a distance and daydreaming about *what-ifs* and the future she hoped for. I watch my mother run barefoot out our front door to hug her own when she comes to visit and I am reminded that this is also her — a human being, someone's little girl, so much more than the title *mother* allowed her to be.

Lung Capacity

Sometimes I wish I could've had the opportunity to know you as a teenager. Maybe we could have been the sort of friends who swapped wardrobes and wore matching outfits to all of Dad's home games in the fall. Or laughed together until our bellies ached and tears coated our cheeks & spent every summer at each other's houses. We'd apply makeup to each other's faces while blindfolded on your bedroom floor and later eat ice cream right from the cart with the same spoon while watching shitty reality tv with your mom on the sofa. Maybe we'd fight over a boy, a stupid one neither of us even *really* liked. We would have been the sort of friends that were inseparable as children and even more so as young adults finding their way in life. I would have been the godmother to your children and you'd be the first to hold mine and I can't help but think we would've been pretty great together like that.

Lung Capacity

In my next life, I pray to be born again as my mother's mother so I can love her in all the ways she deserved to be but never was. I'd handle her with gentle hands and speak to her with only kindness embedded in my voice. I'd braid her hair before school, and make her heart-shaped pancakes for breakfast each morning served with cheery good mornings and a soft kiss on the top of her head.

I will be the mother my mother deserved as a little girl in my next life.

I will hold her when she cries. Brush her teeth and clean her room when her body no longer possesses the energy to do such simple tasks. I will welcome every version of her home with open arms and a heart ready to learn how to love this new side of her. She will never have to fear facing judgment within her own home. She will grow in a house filled with unconditional love and warmth, and maybe then, when she is older, she will understand how easy it is to love her.

Lung Capacity

I'm my father's daughter.

I'm his soft eyes and sharp tongue.
I'm the kindness he carries inside his pocket
and the anger he throws at walls
at the smallest inconveniences.

I am my father's daughter,
hurricanes and the innocence of a soaring butterfly.
Sometimes being his makes me an admirable person,
and other times it makes me a woman
filled with rage with an unknown cause
just like her father.

Mae Setrova

Lung Capacity

I want to rip my heart out of my chest
and show you the damage.
I want to force you to look at it.
To look at the horror you've created,
the unfixable mess you made.

Look at how you've ruined me
before I even had a chance.

Lung Capacity

Tell me you know what you did.
I don't need you to say you're sorry,
I don't want the apology you don't mean.
I just want your acknowledgment.

I want you to take accountability for it.
I want you to look me in the eye, Mom,
and tell me you understand the ways you
failed one child for the protection of another.

I don't need an apology.
Don't tell me you're sorry, I'm tired of hearing
you repeat words you do not mean.
Just look at me and tell me you know
what you've done and didn't care.

Tell me you knew what you were doing
but did it anyway.

Mae Setrova

Lung Capacity

I want to scream at you,
I want to rip your hair out
and pound on your chest and
yell *"How could you"* until I'm blue in the face
and my lungs collapse.

I want to seek out answers for the things
you did to me and let happen.
I want to hate you for it all,
but in my heart is a little girl that just whispers
"I forgive you" when I want to scream that I hate you.

Lung Capacity

But I didn't need just anyone's support.
I needed yours.

Theirs didn't matter to me,
not like yours did.
I just needed you to tell me I could do it,
that you were proud of me and would always
be in my corner no matter what
but you didn't say any of that.

You didn't say a word.

Lung Capacity

I want to scream
"Where the hell were you when I needed you?!"
but you were right there the entire time,
and you didn't give a shit about me.

Lung Capacity

How can I hate you and love you
in the same breath?
What is this inability to look at you
and feel nothing when that is what you deserve?
this curse of always carrying you somewhere
between my bones regardless of what you do.

I love you and I am unable to ever stop.

Lung Capacity

There used to be a time when I thought my parents were infinite. That they would be around for the rest of my life and see me through every stage of it but that isn't true.

One day I'm going to wake up and they aren't going to be here. I'll never smell my dad's cooking again or feel my mother's arms around my shoulders. I won't get to ask them questions I have yet to learn the answers to and they will no longer be just a phone call away from me or right down the hall. I will have to grieve the loss of them one day at a time without my mom to tell me it's going to be okay or my dad to lean on. I will only have memories and how is that ever going to be enough?

Lung Capacity

I'm scared that if I have children
I will become like my parents.

Full of regret for all the things I never
took the time to become and sad
because the life I have is not the one I want.

Lung Capacity

"A lady shouldn't be so angry" they would say to me in disapproval as if this rage wasn't passed down to me from entire generations built off of it.

I was an angry child that grew into an angry woman and a woman that carries this kind of rage around is difficult to want or love. I was a girl with anger identical to my father's, the only difference was his labeled him a man and mine made me crazy.

Lung Capacity

I forgive you.

Not for your own peace of mind but for mine.
I forgive you for me, Mom.
For everything you did and everything you didn't.
I have carried this anger with me long enough
to know I deserve to put it down and walk away from it.
I deserve to feel this sort of relief
even if it wasn't earned,
even if it isn't deserved or owed to you.

I forgive you for everything
you never apologized for, Mom.
I forgive you for not being what
or who I needed.

Lung Capacity

It was never supposed to be my job to take care of you.

You were the parent. *You* were supposed to comfort *me*, to take care of me and love me and protect me, not the other way around. I was meant to be the child, not the adult but that is exactly what you forced me to be with your carelessness.

I was not supposed to be the caregiver to the people that gave me life and yet I was, and I never even got so much as an *"I'm sorry"* for it or a simple thank you for everything I did.

Lung Capacity

"Be the bigger person and forgive them"

I will do no such thing.
I will scream and shout and cry hysterically about it.
I will tell the world what was done to me
and I will make them listen even when
they don't want to hear it.
I won't forgive them, not for this.
Not after all this destruction.

I will not be silenced for someone else's
comfort any longer.

Lung Capacity

"I hope you have a daughter just like you" my mother would shout at me like my existence was a form of punishment instead of a gift and she wanted me to know the anguish she felt at the sight of me.

"I hope you have a daughter just like you" but I did Mom, and she has my same loud laugh and a mind full of questions to ask. She loves to be held, and the color pink and she is filled to the brim with emotions ready to spew out of her. She is exactly like me, Mom. She is everything I could have been if you loved me this way, and loving her is the easiest thing in this world that I have ever done.

Lung Capacity

My mother stands in the mirror and tears herself down then an hour later she tells me how I look just like her.

As a little girl, my mother was the most beautiful woman in the world and being told I look like her made me feel beautiful, too. But after years of watching her degrade and insult all the parts of her that are identical to those same parts of me, I'm no longer sure if her saying I look just like her is meant to be kind.

Does she view me the way she views herself?

Lung Capacity

When I say that I am afraid of being my father or making my mother's mistakes, I am greeted with the old saying *"The apple doesn't fall far from the tree"* as if I am destined to be just like them solely because I am a product of them.

I want to tell them that the apple can roll away.
That it can hit the ground running and drift away with the creek's stream. That it can be picked up by gentle hands and placed somewhere different, a better place where the apple is polished and admired and painted like it's art.

"The apple still came from the tree" they'll argue.

But it can feel different, *be* different.
The apple doesn't have to go far in order to be nothing like the rest of the tree. My exterior may look like theirs but I am not filled with their rot.

Lung Capacity

To my child(ren): I'm sorry.
I don't know if I'll be a good mother and that is why you won't exist.

I'm unsure if I'll always speak to you with the kindness I hope for or if the anger I inherited from my father is buried too deeply within me to ever handle you with softness and the gentle touch of a loving mother.

Our family is built off angry men too prideful to be kind fathers and insecure women with voices too quiet to be women who break the cycle. I can't be what you need me to be, and I don't want to pass this legacy on to anyone else.

It ends with me.
I'm sorry you won't exist.

Mae Setrova

Lung Capacity

One heart begins to beat for two and a single body starts to build another — ten fingers and ten toes, organs that will grow and bones that will break apart & form together again. A set of lungs work overtime to breathe enough for us both and my stomach makes room for you to play. You are born, my body the reason you take your first breath — your heart an extension of my own. I created your fingernails, the hair on your head and your soft skin. How can I hate my body when it has created something so incredible? Something so magical — an entire human being. *You.*

Lung Capacity

Lung Capacity

For the heart that still bleeds

heartbreak, letting go & healing.

Lung Capacity

It's been three weeks since you left.
I can't sit still but I can't seem to find
the strength to move either.
My clothes are piling in the corner,
and my room is exactly how you left it.

I can't bring myself to move a thing.
It's like time has stilled within these four walls
and you're still here.
To change its state is to accept
that you aren't coming back
and I'm not ready to let go just yet.

Mae Setrova

Lung Capacity

My alarm goes off,
it's 6 am and I search for your warmth
under the cover but it's not there.

All I find waiting for me are cold sheets
and an emptiness that your body used to fill.

Lung Capacity

It's October again and you are here — the memory of you in the barren trees and steaming cups of tea.

I worry that the love of our lives isn't always someone we get to spend an eternity with but merely a handful of moments and I wonder how many great love stories must end like this: with torn heartstrings and wounds refusing to heal even after decades. When I say your name, will it always cut my heart back open and cause it to bleed?

Will October ever be just October again or will it always be a reminder of you?

Lung Capacity

If you ever find yourself homesick for me, know that I still keep a spare key hidden beneath the flower pot by the back door.

Don't hesitate to come back, walk right in and sit next to me on the couch as if you never left. Pick out a movie for us to watch. I'll make buttered popcorn and pour our drinks. I won't ask you to explain. I won't acknowledge the absence of you all these months or your sudden reappearance. Instead, I will ask you if you still prefer Dr. Pepper over Coke and if you'd like to order takeout for dinner.

Don't be afraid to come home to me. I am still here. I've been waiting to hear the back door unlock since the day you left through the front.

Lung Capacity

I didn't cry that day because I was sad. I cried because we had no other choice but to walk away from each other. We had run our course. We had to part ways even though it wasn't what either of us wanted because it was the right thing to do. I cried because we held onto each other for dear life but it didn't make a difference in the end. I cried because this was our reality and there were no others we could step into to escape this fate and continue loving. I cried because that was it, the end of our road and our presence in each other's lives. I cried because we were so in love but it wasn't enough to make it work. We were the right people for each other but we did it so terribly wrong that there was no fixing it, not even with time. I cried for us, for what I knew could have been — *should have been.* I cried so much that day and every day after.

Lung Capacity

But what if I didn't want the fucking world?

What if I didn't *want* better or *deserve* better?
What if all I wanted was you?
And all the bullshit that came with you
but you wouldn't let me love you like that
because you didn't feel deserving of it?

What then?
Would you have stayed?
Would it have made a difference
in your decision to leave?
or did it not matter what the hell *I* wanted?

Lung Capacity

If parallel universes do exist,
I hope there is at least one where you come home
with takeout and tell me about your day
in between commercial breaks of our favorite movies
and everything is okay.

Mae Setrova

Lung Capacity

I want to write a pretty poem about all the different ways you broke my heart and make the aftermath sound beautiful. I want to say that the morning after sunlight seeped through the blinds and sun rays danced across the floor. I want to add small details, like the way my sheets still smelled like you after two weeks, and the cup you filled with water three days before was still resting on my nightstand a month after it happened but I don't know if you'd even care. The flowers you last bought me wilted, then molded and my mother had to beg me to throw them out and I cried hysterically when tying the trash bag with them inside. That is how hard I clung to everything you left behind and that is not poetic, that is devastating. That is grieving the living. You left and I held onto everything that remained of you.

Lung Capacity

I never would've left, you know.
I would have stayed and stuck it out without a single complaint.

I would've let you keep abusing my heart just as long as it meant I got to love you a little bit longer in the process. I didn't have it in me to walk away from you, not even when I pleaded with myself to leave. I would've waited it out and hoped for the day you would finally change even if that day never came but you walked away before we ever got to find out and you did it so easily.

Did I ever matter to you the way you mattered to me?

Lung Capacity

How do I let go of the living
and not grieve their absence?

You are alive.
You are healthy and living and yet still,
I am filled with so much grief.

Lung Capacity

Do I walk away from this
or grab hold of it with both hands?
Do I forget you, or wait a lifetime for your return?

When will the tears I still cry for you stop being sympathized with and be seen as a refusal to move on? I don't know how to let go of you, not yet. I don't know when I am expected to set us down and allow what we were to be nothing more than a piece of the past. I wait for you to reach out and confess that you feel this way too but you are not there anymore. There is only the sound of my heart breaking and your continued silence. When will I stop searching for you in places you have never been and people you've never met?

How do I walk away from something I still want?
How do I walk away from *you?*

Lung Capacity

I want to reach out. I want to send you every insignificant thought that crosses my mind the way I once did and have you dissect every hidden meaning within each sentence I speak until you know me right down to my bones again. You do not miss me, I know this. You do not want to hear from me ever again, I know this too, but I wish you did. I wish you struggled as much as I do to not drive to your house and pretend we never ended, to sit down on the edge of your bed and not acknowledge the year-long gap in our memories where we can't find pieces of each other as you turn on a show we forgot to finish. I want to live in oblivion like that, in a distorted reality where I dissociated while drying dishes after dinner with your parents and none of this ever took place, and when I turned to look for you I'd find you resting against the kitchen counter peeling an orange for me to eat the way you always did. I miss you, to say that doesn't even begin to capture the despair your absence has brought me but I will cling to this ache because it's all I have left of you — that and the pain that grows each time your name is murmured in my presence.

Lung Capacity

An afternoon in mid-June and your car pulls into my driveway the same way it has been for the past year, only today is different because it's the last time I'll ever see it here. I carry a camo green duffel bag out containing the rest of your belongings within it and my cheeks are damp from the time I spent crying while packing it. You step out with damp cheeks of your own and pull me into a hug. You grab fistfuls of my sweater like you never want to let me go but that's exactly what we're doing here.

"We weren't supposed to say goodbye to each other" I cried into your shoulder and you held me a little bit tighter. *"Just because we're letting go doesn't mean we want to"* you whispered.

Lung Capacity

I remember every last detail of your face.
Right down to the freckle behind your left ear
and the stories behind the scars you carry
but I don't have a clue what words would come out of your
mouth if we were to ever speak again.

You are a stranger I would recognize anywhere.

Lung Capacity

I would have let you break my heart
a million different times if it meant
you would love me just a little bit longer.

I would have let you completely ruin me
if that was what it took to have an extra five minutes
spent in your presence.

Lung Capacity

Come home to me. Come home and tell me everything I did wrong during our time together. Come home and fight with me again. Come home and laugh with me, tell me bad jokes and fold the towels wrong the way you always did. Come home and tell me about your day, your shitty coworkers and your even worse boss. Come home and hold me again, scream at me if you need to. I don't care what we do. I don't care if it ends again, just come home, please. And love me just a little while longer.

Lung Capacity

I turned my Snapchat recaps off a few weeks after we ended.

I know this doesn't sound all that sad or moving but I couldn't seem to erase you from everything. I spent hours deleting every photo and video of you I could find but I couldn't delete your shadow from them. You were there in each one, physically or just a hand, a laugh in the background, just the dashboard of a car I no longer sit in the passenger side of so I turned my recaps off, and I don't think I'll ever go back into my settings in search of a way to turn it back on.

Lung Capacity

I wonder if ghosts are jealous
of the way you haunt me
while still living.

Lung Capacity

There's a post on Facebook floating around saying the cells in the human body begin to replace themselves every 7 years and I don't know how true this statement is but I do know that if it is, I will wake up one day in a body that doesn't know you anymore. I will be in a body that you've never held or seen undressed or even kissed and it will never know that you are a missing detail.

I'm terrified that if there is no longer a cell in this body that has known yours, the rest of me will begin to erase you too, and I will have lost you twice in one lifetime.

Lung Capacity

Tell me to stay.
Tell me you made a mistake letting me go.
That my absence makes it hard for you to breathe.
Tell me you regret ever saying goodbye to me.

Confess that you still hope for me to come back,
tell me I'm home in the form of a person
and that without me, life is bleak.

Tell me you still need me.
Beg for me not to go.
Cry for me to come back and promise me
this time, you really will change.

Please, ask me to stay.

Lung Capacity

I killed myself that evening after you left. Blood did not spill onto the floor or stain the rug beneath my feet but I still died. My lungs still collapsed and my heart still stopped before deciding to beat again as someone new, someone you didn't love and who never loved you. I held a silent funeral in my room for her that night — the girl I was with you and knew I never would be again. I said a quick eulogy and shoved her body into my closet. Nobody noticed her absence at the dinner table or questioned the smell of despair reeking from my bedroom. You were gone and so was she and I was the only person grieving the people who died the night we said goodbye to each other.

Lung Capacity

You are a ghost that starts to haunt me at the start of August and infects every small thing about winter. You're in the smell of pumpkin spice candles and the taste of green tea. You're brown leaves crunching on gravel roads, lamp posts decorated for Halloween on small-town streets, and flower beds filled with wilted daffodils. I catch glimpses of your face in my hot cocoa and in windows during holiday shopping. You're in the smell of freshly baked apple pies on Thanksgiving day and warm oatmeal raisin cookies. When the wind blows and the air is crisp, I hear your name being whispered by the trees rubbing together and the crackle of a fire. You are in everything after summer and before spring.

Lung Capacity

I wish I could go back to the night we met
and study you a little more closely.
I wish I had taken in your every feature a little better and
wrote down every word we spoke to each other that evening
knowing what I know now.

That you will leave, and every part of you I've come to love
will fade away with time and I'll be left with nothing but a
forgetful mind and an aching heart that desperately wants to
remember.

Lung Capacity

Just once, I want to be the one who is missed by someone.

I want to be the one who is cried over
and impossible to forget.
I want to be a sensitive topic for someone
and told repeatedly about how deeply
my absence is felt.
I want poems to be written about me
and a heart to ache over me.

Just once I want my absence to bother someone.
I'm tired of being the one who is left
and can't ever let go.

Lung Capacity

I have a confession: *you still feel like home.*

After everything, after all this time,
you still feel like home.
Like warmth and safety
and contentment.

I try to deny it but it doesn't change the fact
that it's true. You are still home to me
and I wish you would come back
because I ache to be there again.

Lung Capacity

I still love you.

I still remember your favorite color and I still have your birthday pinned in my calendar. I remember the shampoo you used to use and the exact kind of deodorant you wore like it is a necessary piece of information to carry with me. I remember all of your tattoos, and the exact placement of each one and all the ones you wished to get but never did. I remember you. I remember every small detail about you. I still know your pant size, and dreams, and your Taco Bell order, and your favorite brand of shoe.

The love I had for you is still here and it refuses to ever leave.

Lung Capacity

I remember the first time you ever hit me.

Your apology came quickly after. Four *"I'm sorry's"* in a row so close together I couldn't hear the emptiness hidden within them. You held me with hands draped in false gentleness as you begged me for forgiveness. *"It'll never happen again,"* you promised at least a hundred times.

I should've known better. I spent years watching women escape men just like you, promising myself I would never be in their position and there I stood, directly in their shoes and I forgave you that time and at least a thousand times after. It took me so long to leave.

Why is it so hard to leave men like you?

Lung Capacity

I hate you so much.

I hate you for what you did to me and for who you've become and for being impossible to forget. I hate that it's been years and my heart still sinks every time I find out you've been with someone else even though it's no longer my right to be this upset about it. I hate you for making it look so easy to walk away from us while I'm still clinging to every broken piece I can find because I can't let go. I hate that even when I say I hate you, I can't bring myself to mean it. I hate you for being someone I'll always love no matter what you do or how much time passes by. I hate that I can't hate you, even when I try to.

Lung Capacity

"She didn't mean anything"
How dare you say that as if it's meant to make this better,
easier.

Don't sit there and tell me she meant nothing to you because
she still made you throw everything away just for one night
with her. Telling me she meant nothing to you is an insult, it's
a slap to the face so don't sit there and use those words like a
bandaid when they are salt poured into an open wound.

"she meant nothing"
but the cost of being with her was everything.

Lung Capacity

Come home.

Let your feet carry you back to me.
Take your shoes off at the front door and place your keys
in the little glass bowl on the kitchen counter.
Drape your coat over the back of a dining room chair
and take your socks off at the foot of the bed next to the cat.
Climb under the white sheets with me — kiss me softly and
say that today, you missed me. Tell me about your week as I
drift off to sleep and kiss my cheek softly before you
inevitably go when the sun begins to rise.

Come home to me.
Even if it's only momentarily.
Even if you do not stay, just come home,
and let these hands hold you again.

Lung Capacity

Everyone I know has an unforgettable love story over the course of summer but ours began in the fall and now every time I see those pumpkin patch posts start to flood my Facebook feed, I know the ghost of what we almost were is just around the corner.

Lung Capacity

He said he loved me with porn infesting his browser history.

He doesn't understand why that little fact taints those three words he swears to me he means. No man ever does. *"I don't want those women, I want you!"* But when I undress myself in front of him he stares at me the same way he stares at them and I can no longer see the difference between us.

I can't tell if he really loves me for me or just the convenience of having me there.

Lung Capacity

He says he loves me with half-naked strangers on his social media feed and doesn't understand why intimacy is something I no longer crave.

I don't know if this is really love anymore, or just his fear of being alone.

Lung Capacity

"I didn't know how to love you"
but it didn't matter how.

It didn't matter how you chose to love me because no matter how you did it, it would have been enough. You could have put it in a different language and I would have learned to speak it. To read and write it, I would've learned it better than I know my own.

I just wanted your love in any form you'd give it to me. I would have relished any amount of it and made it be enough for me. It didn't matter how you loved me and you knew that. You just didn't want to and you're too much of a coward to say it.

Lung Capacity

I think that for the rest of my life,
I will always have a love for you that refuses to die out.

It will be here regardless of what I do to rid of it
or the amount of time spent in silence that passes between us.
I think this will be the most pure form of love
I will ever get to experience in this lifetime
and the thought of that crushes me because I know
that's not what I am to you.

Lung Capacity

I want to fall in love again.
I want to be infatuated with another
human being who isn't you anymore
but I am bored of each one I meet.

They don't excite me the way you used to,
they don't make me feel the things you did
or love me in the same ways and I can't seem to stop
comparing them to the way you were.
They could learn every last detail about me
and I'd still wonder if you remember them too.

I want to fall in love with someone else.
Someone who isn't you but all I seem to do
is want them to be you.

Lung Capacity

Do you ever think about me from time to time and think, *"I wonder what she's doing right now. I wonder if she is happy while she does it"*

Because I do. I wonder about you all the time. I wonder if you are doing well, if your favorite color has remained the same or if you have taken up a new hobby. I wonder if you have met someone new and fallen in love with them, and I try to find a rational reason for that thought still causing an ache somewhere between my ribs. I want to call you sometimes, just to hear your voice and see if time has changed the way you sound.

I know you wouldn't answer if I ever did try to call but there's a tiny part of me that says *"But what if he does."* I don't know what it would mean if you did, and I don't know what I would say after all this time of silence.

Lung Capacity

I miss you.

I don't just say that to have something to talk about, I really mean it and sometimes I think you miss me too but neither of us will ever say it or admit it to the other. I'll keep trying to let you go believing that's what you really want and you'll keep thinking I deserve something you're incapable of being so you'll never come back and we'll never speak again.

We'll spend the rest of this life fighting the urge to go back to each other believing that's what the other wants because we're both too scared of what the other outcome could be.

Lung Capacity

I will never allow myself to forget
the way I sat on cold bathroom tiles
clutching a white towel around my body
as I held every broken piece of myself in my hands
trying to figure out how to put them back together
again.

Lung Capacity

I wanted to go through this life together.
In all its extraordinary forms and simplicity,
I wanted it all with you.

The good and the bad. I would've gone through hell and come back just to do it all over again as long as it was you I came back to. You were my heaven on earth, a sanctuary safe from home when home wasn't safe to be around anymore. You were stability in a life built off shaky grounds and uncertainty.

I wanted to go through the rest of this life with you.
I wanted *everything* with you.

Lung Capacity

I hope time really does
take this feeling away.

Lung Capacity

Every time something exciting happens to me or I accomplish something I've always talked about, I have to fight the urge to call you and tell you about it.

I wanna tell you everything that's happened this past year, every last detail but that's not my place anymore. You're no longer the person I tell everything to and I'm still trying to be okay with that.

Lung Capacity

I wish I could let you go
the same way you've let go of me.

I wish I could walk away as easily,
and set all this leftover love down
and never pick it up again
but I can never seem to stop coming back to it
in hopes I'll find you there resting against it
ready to try with me again.

Lung Capacity

I think I'm the girl before the wife. The one that teaches them how to be kind men and that loving a girl openly and strongly is not a weakness their high school friends made it out to be. I'm the experience — the one they have many firsts with and paves the way through territory not yet tread on so that when the right girl does come along, they don't completely screw it up the first week. I give them entertaining stories to tell and a girl to talk about when the topic of first loves comes up during a date and maybe, just maybe the cause of the wife's insecurity that she was not the first instead of me because even though she is the one he chose, I was still something to him that she could never be.

I think I'm the girl before the wife and I worry I always will be. *Something special but not enough to keep.*

Lung Capacity

"Do you think you'll always be this in love with him?"

"I think that even when I am on my deathbed he'll still cross my mind, and when fear of the unknown comes for me I'll reach for every memory of him that comes"

Lung Capacity

I went out with friends last night
and in the midst of it all, I thought of you.

I worry that you'll follow me everywhere
I go for the rest of my life.
That even when I am laughing with my friends
and feel happiness without you,
I will still think of you and wish this feeling
was something you still wanted to share with me.

Lung Capacity

2:13 am

I'm watching you try to drink the memory of me away on a video taken by a once mutual friend and I see the moment it hits you — *I will always be there.* You can drink all the alcohol you want and you will still remember everything about me. My laugh, the way I smile, my favorite ice cream flavor, the way your t-shirts used to fit me. There isn't enough alcohol in the world to make you forget me and you know it.

You can't drink me away, and I won't wait for you to be sober.

Lung Capacity

I was 15 when I stumbled upon love for the first time in my life that wasn't tied to family or friendships forged during kindergarten recess. This was the kind of love that lingered in your chest and bloomed curious thoughts you had never felt the need to conjure before. The first longing to make your chest ache and your vocal cords fail to properly work in their presence. He was my first love which meant I could love without fear of the unknown because my heart had never been broken so I didn't know the pain a love like this could bring once it reached the end.

Sometimes, I wonder what life would look like if I could love that way again.

Lung Capacity

Love me for a lifetime or do not love me at all.

I don't want to be a chapter in your life,
just a short story you tell your children
when they ask about the women you loved
before their mother.

I am tired of being only a story,
a memory for people to think back on
and nothing more than that.
So I am begging you, love me for a lifetime
or do not bother loving me at all.

Lung Capacity

Don't chase after my heart just to let it go.
Don't do that to me like everyone else has.
Please, don't make me fall in love with you
knowing you aren't going to stay
once the honeymoon stage comes to an end
and you realize how difficult this really is.

Lung Capacity

I will not text you and tell you I miss you.

I won't drunk dial your number a hundred times until you answer and I won't ask your friends about how you're doing, no matter how much I may want to or try to force my way back into your life. I know there's no room for me there anymore.

I won't do any of these things, no matter how tempting they may be but I'll go to sleep every night silently praying it will be disrupted at 4:19 am with a drunk dial from you and 56 unread messages all saying the same thing —— *I miss you, I'm sorry.*

Lung Capacity

I have loved you twice. I don't mean across different lifetimes, I mean in this very one.

I have loved you once as you laid across from me with messy hair and sunlight shining across your face. I loved you during arguments filled with misunderstandings and anger and on slow Sunday mornings made up of our laughter and half-finished Netflix episodes.

And I love you again as I watch you live a life void of me. As I watch you fall in love with other people and slowly forget about me. I love you now at a distance, knowing too much to be a stranger and having the sort of history that doesn't allow us to be *just* friends.

In this life, I have loved you twice. I have loved you while you were mine and I love you again while you're not.

Lung Capacity

I get your coffee order sometimes when I miss you. I know it sounds silly but I haven't seen you in months and I know the chances of me ever seeing you again are next to nothing so sometimes when I still ache to be near you, I go down to my local cafe and I order the same drink you always got. This coffee is a way for me to still have a little piece of your presence when your absence is all that I'm allowed to have.

Lung Capacity

I hope you never manage to forget me.

I hope my name claws at the inside of your throat like a sentence you desperately need to get out but can't. I hope it burns every time you try to swallow it like it has no meaning.

I hope everything you come to love finds a way to remind you of me, and I hope your mom still slips up sometimes and says my name by accident and it nearly kills you to hear it.

I pray my memory has stained your entire life and each time you try to scrub it out it only spreads. I hope you never forget me, or what you did.

Lung Capacity

We run into each other unexpectedly at a crowded mall and like any pair of strangers with a shared past we stir up small talk. I ask you how your mom has been and you tell me she's good, that she misses me and I say I think of her all the time. You ask me if I'm still writing and I show you some of my poetry — you tell me they're incredible and that I've always had a brilliant mind and I smile because I haven't received a compliment that mattered to me since the day we last spoke. You tell me you have to go and I want to tell you to stay right then, to reach for your hand and ask you to walk alongside me and tell me everything I've missed all this time apart and when you pause without reason before turning to go, I wonder for a moment if you wanted that too.

Lung Capacity

Sept 7th.
I miss you

Sept 30th.
I went on a date tonight.
he wasn't anything like you.

Oct 14th.
Do you miss me sometimes?

Nov 7th.
Happy birthday!!

Nov 10th.
I found one of your old shirts while doing laundry.
I think I'll wear it to bed tonight.

Dec 25th.
Merry Christmas!

Feb 17th.
I saw your new girlfriend. She's really pretty.

March 24th.
Maybe in another life, huh?

Lung Capacity

I miss when your name didn't make my chest ache.

When it was just one of those things you heard a mother shout from time to time in public spaces but held no significance to me.

I miss when I didn't know you. When my eyes didn't scan every room I entered in hopes I'd find you there standing among strangers just to feel disappointment when you aren't there to be found.

Lung Capacity

Hold me the way one would hold a grudge — fiercely, like your life depends on your ability to cling to it. With fists clenched so tight your fingers ache and your knuckles turn white.

Hold me with the intent of keeping me like a secret. Clutched to your heart and held with purpose. Let my name be a story you're dying to tell and speak it everywhere you go — talk of me so much I become an unseen piece of your identity.

Lung Capacity

When we first ended, people kept telling me it would get easier with time. That my pain would subside and you would become nothing more than a fond memory I speak of from time to time when I'm older but I think they were wrong because this doesn't seem to get any easier as time slips on without you. You are still a person I know every detail about.

Your name is still a bruise that hurts to touch.

Lung Capacity

Take your time coming back to me.

Really, I mean it.
I want you to go and do everything
you couldn't with me at your side,
no matter what that may entail.

Don't be in a rush to come back,
I promise I'll still be here when you're ready
to come find me again and I swear that this time,
we'll do things right.

Lung Capacity

If I could go back in time, back to the day we met I would do it all over again with you. I know we didn't make it. I know I can't change our ending because it wasn't the mistakes we made that did it, it was us. We weren't right for each other but if given the chance to go back to the day it all started and handed the opportunity to walk away instead, I would still choose to love you regardless of this.

Lung Capacity

A friend of mine asked me what happened between us after we ended and I couldn't answer her question, not even when I thought about it because truthfully, I didn't know.

It wasn't something we saw coming or suspected.
We just woke up one morning and felt like strangers sleeping next to each other and neither of us knew when or how it had happened.

I think that was the saddest part about it really. The way we planned an entire life together and without warning, we stopped being the people we saw in it. The love we shared for each other was just there the week prior and it had vanished without so much as a trace of where it had gone and that was it, the end of what we had and all of the dreams we shared.

Lung Capacity

I've loved so many people in this lifetime
but none of them came as easily as loving you.

It came to me like an instinct, like second nature — something
I have done a hundred times before and knew from memory
alone. It were as if I was made to do this. Like my existence
was created solely to love yours and nobody else's.

Maybe this has been my purpose through every life I've lived
and that is why walking away from you is so hard to do.

Lung Capacity

I want to grow old with you.

I want to bathe in our youth completely in love and full of life and watch as our skin begins to fade of its color as the years go by. I dream of waking up next to you in our 70s, skin wrinkled and matching laugh lines beneath our eyes and a hallway with every vacant space filled with framed photographs of the life we built and shared together.

When this life is over, I pray it ends next to you in a soft king-size bed and your hand tucked into mine.

Lung Capacity

And each time you achieve a goal,
every time you reach a dream of yours
and a milestone you thought you never would,
I hope you can hear my applause and feel my genuine
happiness.

I know we do not speak anymore
but I still cheer you on from a safe distance.
I am still in your corner rooting for you
even if you can't see me standing here anymore.

Lung Capacity

We'll never come back to one another.
I know that now.

I'm not meant for you
and you're not meant for me,
but I'll carry you and all of our memories
with me until it's time to meet again
in the next life.

Lung Capacity

<u>4:17 A.M.</u>

Hey.

I glance at the text. I ignore it. I fight the urge to open it, to text you back and fall into your trap. You're not texting me because you miss me. You aren't reaching out to me because you love me and want to fix things. You're texting me because it's 4:17 in the morning and you're lonely and want me to fill the void.

I know that if I respond, you will say you miss me. You will ask me to come over and I'll end up right where I started — trying to find a way to leave you that doesn't leave me in a million pieces. Instead, I'll go to bed alone tonight and by morning, you will have forgotten about me.

Lung Capacity

The silence I keep between us is not my unsaid confession that I don't love you anymore.

It is my attempt at telling you it's okay to leave.
That you can go now and be everything you ever wanted.

I will be okay without you, I will find a way to be so go, and leave the guilt you carry behind.

Lung Capacity

You are not foolish for loving that man or that woman as strongly as you did, or for believing every word they ever spoke to you. You were so in love with them and you rightfully thought they were in love, too. You aren't foolish for giving them a second chance after they so badly messed up the first one. They promised you change in such a convincing way, how could you not believe them or their pleas for forgiveness? You aren't foolish for still thinking about them either, for still crying over them and holding out hope that they really will change one day and come back for you. It meant so much — what you had with them.

None of it makes you foolish.
Their inability to love you does not determine
your ability to be loved.

Lung Capacity

I saw a quote a few weeks ago that said everyone has an almost and I haven't been able to stop thinking about it since because I think that's what you are to me.

My *almost*.

You were my person but you were not mine to keep. Only to hold, only to love for a short while then let go. You were almost it, the person I would have spent forever with without hesitation but that dream was never ours to have, was it? We were always built on borrowed time and I was foolish to think otherwise.

I think that will always haunt me in some kind of way. The things we almost got to become together. We wanted the stars and infinity but all we got was *almost*.

Lung Capacity

I keep waiting for you to come back, and I keep thinking that when — *if* you do, we could go back to the way things used to be but I know better. Deep down, in the pit of my stomach and the center of my bones, I know that if you ever came back you wouldn't be the same person you were the day I lost you. You would be someone else, an entirely different person that I know nothing about. You will never be the person you were with me again and that is who I miss.

Lung Capacity

Find me again somewhere down the road of life.

When we are older and wiser and have learned how to love a little bit better. Collect new memories like tiny treasures and tell me all about them several years from now when you run into me at a local fair.

We'll start again there, as new people ready to try again.

Lung Capacity

My last relationship was the one I wanted to work. It was the one I hoped would, and poured all of myself into to ensure it bloomed in hopes that I would never have to be without him again but love wasn't enough to build forever off of. I thought he was it, *my person.* The better half of myself, even the rest of my life but he wasn't. He was only a person passing through it but I still prayed he would turn out to be something more than that. He was the best thing that ever happened to me but something I was only meant to experience, not keep. A love I will think back on for the rest of my life and always have *what-ifs* about.

Lung Capacity

I hope our love lasts in at least one
version of our lives where we meet.

Lung Capacity

I miss you. Not in the sort of way that makes me call you at 3 am and beg for answers, or want you back. I miss you in the kind of way that makes me hope we run into each other somewhere so I can tell you I still fold my towels the way you showed me and I still listen to all the songs you introduced me to. I miss you in the kind of way that means I will carry parts of you with me for the rest of my life. Bits of your vocabulary and the way your arm would rest on the center console while driving. I wish I could tell you that.

I wish you knew what you've given me without trying.

Mae Setrova

Lung Capacity

I don't think you were my greatest love anymore.
I think I was just 16 and in love with the idea of it.
I don't think it was as good as I remember it to be either, you
weren't this amazing man I made you out to be, and accepting
that has been the hardest part of healing from this.

Lung Capacity

We can move on but we will still always remember, won't we?

I met someone. He is kind and he has soft eyes. He's good to me, this new boy with golden locks of hair but I still think of you and the smell of your old spice shampoo.

He took me to a park for our first unofficial date. We drank apple juice boxes and split a nacho Lunchable on the wooden park bench while we talked about our pasts. I saw a memory of us play out on the swing sets when taking wood chips out of my shoes and my chest ached for what used to be.

He's good to me, this new boy with pools of honey in his eyes. I tell myself he is enough for me but he is not you and I fear that small fact will make me doubt everyone who dares to love me after you.

Lung Capacity

Stop waiting for them to come back.
they aren't going to, at least not in this lifetime
and maybe not even in the next one.
You have to stop begging people to stay
when they ask to leave and do so willingly.
You can't keep holding onto people that aren't yours
to hold onto.

They left.
They made their choice and have found peace
in the ending and there's nothing you can do to change it.
It's time for you to let go, too.

Lung Capacity

We don't make it, do we?

Not in this life and not even in the next. We don't create a beautiful love story filled with dream houses and children with green eyes & blonde hair or handwritten love letters read to each other underneath a white oak tree. We are not built for life-long devotion and old age sitting in rocking chairs on warm August nights. We are a short story, a mere paragraph to each other. We're memories that ache to remember and nothing more than that. The purpose of us was to fall in love only to fall out of it, that is all this was ever meant to be — a love only meant to serve as a lesson.

Lung Capacity

I think the part that hurt the most was the realization that I miss a person who no longer exists.

You have the same facial features and the same stride, even the same voice and the same interests but you are not the you I miss and only I can see the difference between who you are and who you once were.

The man you used to be left without a sound, without any warning. He didn't bother to explain his reasons for leaving and that is what hurts me the most

Lung Capacity

When closure finds me, I will relish in its warmth. I will let it take my hand and lead me onto better things and away from the *what-ifs* I have spent the last few years clinging onto. I'll let the rose-colored lenses fall to the floor and welcome the reality of you they have kept hidden away from me.

When closure finds me, I will greet it with a smile. I will write down the feeling of finding it and I will fall in love with not being in love.

Lung Capacity

"What if I never heal from this"
a younger version of me sobs on her bedroom floor.

I want to reach out and wipe the tears from her cheeks. I want to whisper *"But you will"* into her ear and stand in front of her as living proof that her broken heart will mend with time. It may take us years, many months of nights crying and supermarket runs avoiding certain aisles but it heals, bit by bit without you ever realizing it's happening.

We get over him, and we never look back.

Lung Capacity

Lung Capacity

For the wounded minds

mental health, grief.

Lung Capacity

You asked me how it felt to grieve a few months
after their passing as if time could ever heal this,
and when I told you that their funeral
was the first time I ever *really* wanted to die
and I have longed for death everyday since,
you could no longer look me in the eye.

Lung Capacity

People view the people who muzzle their grief like heartless bastards. Our silence is considered a confession that we never loved the dead the way we claimed when they were living but the truth is we don't know how to speak of it without drowning in the weight of the grief it brings.

Our grief is silent because if we dared to give sound to it, we would never know *quiet* again.

Lung Capacity

I stand on top of the fresh soil marking your grave and for a moment, I catch myself wanting to claw my way through it.

I want to get down on all fours
like some sort of wild animal and dig my way down to you.
I want to rip open the lid of your coffin and cradle myself into your arms again, safely tucked away and hidden from this hurt your death has brought me, and go to whatever heaven or hell you have gone to.

I don't want to be here without you.
I don't know *how* to be here without you.

Lung Capacity

I think the worst part about you being gone is the lack of evidence that you were ever really here to begin with. There is nothing I can reach out and touch to confirm your existence and there is nothing that ties me to you. I don't have any photographs to look back on or text messages to reread a thousand times until I can recite each sentence in them.

All I have is a heaviness in my chest where you used to be.

Lung Capacity

Sometimes I feel like you were only a figment of my imagination from how much I am starting to forget. An imaginary friend of sorts I made up to fill this lonely void I have always had but then I remember there is a headstone out there somewhere with your name on it, and that is the only thing you left behind to show you were ever even here.

Lung Capacity

I dreamt that you were alive again last night
and I know that for the next few days
I am going to cling to every detail of it until my mind
inevitably erases every piece.

Lung Capacity

You died and I desperately need to tell you how it feels. I need you to hold me upright while I show you this hole that exists now in my heart and the emptiness that swallows my soul. I need you to hold me while I cry out for you, and scream at God for an answer I already have but refuse to accept as a reason.

You have died and you are the only one who can get me through it.

Lung Capacity

Your memory is tucked away
in the corners of August
and the smell of autumn rain.

You haunt me in the most
subtle ways.

Lung Capacity

I'm starting to forget you.
How you look,
the sound of your laughter,
the voice I used to know so well.

I hate this part of losing someone.
When so much time passes
that your mind starts to erase parts of them
until you're left with nothing but a blur of memories
you can't really make out anymore.

Lung Capacity

Losing you has taught me that grief
is never just one small thing,
but a thousand of them weighing on you
all at once.

Lung Capacity

A vital part of grieving is forgetting.

This is a lesson I have fought since my first encounter with grief. You will always remember them, that they were here and the role they played in your life but as time slips on without them, you will begin to notice the details fading. You'll remember their laughter but you will struggle to remember the depth of it and their features will start to blur into images you can't quite make out anymore, and there is nothing you can do to stop this from happening.

You will forget, at least some things and that is a part of grief. The love you carry for them will remain and it will be heavy but it is the one thing grief does not dare to take.

Lung Capacity

I feel your absence everywhere.
It's in everything you've left behind
and it is suffocating.

You've gone away but the ghost of you
still lingers here. It's followed me around
since your funeral and I can't seem to get rid of it.
Your absence has made the silence unbearably loud.

Lung Capacity

Don't tell me they're in a better place.

Don't sit there as I cry and grieve this loss
and tell me this is the better outcome
or what they would or wouldn't want me to do
with this hurt. You're not the one who has lost something
so viciously without a single warning.
You're not the one mourning a death that was never
supposed to happen like this so don't pretend to know
what you're talking about when you tell me
this will pass because it won't.

Lung Capacity

I hold your memory with my fists clenched so tightly my fingers turn red and my knuckles become white, afraid that if I loosen my grip every memory I have of you will fly away somewhere out of my reach and I'll no longer remember any of the details.

Lung Capacity

It consumed me — losing you.

The world started to serve only as a reminder of you. Of what I had lost and would never get back so I stopped going out and started to stay in. For weeks after your death I went on like this, hidden away from the world. I was a prisoner confined to my own bed and the only company I had was a photo of you taken years ago with the date of your funeral displayed at the bottom.

I know you wouldn't have wanted this for me but it was hard to continue living without you here to show me how to do it.

Lung Capacity

I died the day you took your last breath.
I died in every single way except physically
but my grief made it feel like maybe I had.

Loss weighed down on my bones so heavily I couldn't breathe from it. It paralyzed me for months on end with no signs of ever letting me escape the feeling it continued to drown me in each night since your funeral.

This ache is slowly killing me.

Lung Capacity

I haven't been the same since you left us.
Grief has done terrible things to me
in your absence.

Lung Capacity

Losing a pet is strange. You were, technically, only a cat. An animal, to some a replaceable thing but I walk around this empty house under my cloud of grief collecting every piece of fur that still remains with the illusion that it will somehow bring you back or make this easier. I glance at a silver bowl still full of your food that will go uneaten and I am unsure of how to go on with my day as if the biggest part of it isn't missing. What do I do with the treats you will never finish or the toys you aren't here to play with any longer?

How do I get people to understand the size of this loss when they have never known this kind of love?

Lung Capacity

Who am I if not a battlefield waiting
for the next war to shake the grounds?
If not a soldier with an open wound
waiting for a medic?

War is the foundation I was built upon.
It wages through my veins
right alongside my blood so I ask you,
who am I if not a man fighting in wars
he did not start and will never see the end of?

What do I become when the war finally stops?

Lung Capacity

On January 1st, I will die the same way I do every new year. I will lay my head on a pillow made of wildflowers in an open meadow and feel my lungs expand for the last time as who I am right now. I'll shed the skin I am wearing, and come spring I will rise again as someone new, someone unrecognizable and I will pluck the first daisy that I see and say hello to passing honey bees. I will mourn myself, the girl I was last January and I'll say my goodbyes in a eulogy I write only in my mind and when it is time, I will walk home and find myself again.

I will miss who I am next year.

Lung Capacity

Who will come to my funeral? Who will visit my grave years after my death and place their bare feet in the grass to feel close to me again? Which strangers will think about me from time to time and grieve for me — an individual they never knew beyond a distance and other people's stories. Will my family decorate my grave? Will they still spend my birthday with me and bring me a whipped cream frosted cupcake with a lit candle in the center or will I be forgotten?

I worry my grave will become another unvisited site that is forgotten and hidden behind grass that hasn't been cut since my burial. Our eternity is the memory of us and I fear that once I die, I will be a forgotten thing.

Lung Capacity

In my dreams, the color of hope is navy blue and feels like cold silk. It's the sound of April rain on warm pavement. The ripple of water clashing against pebbles in a creek and grass tickling your ear when you lie in the backyard to wish upon a shooting star. It's Christmas lights on a white house, a blanket of snow covering power lines and muffling the sounds of the world. In my dreams, hope is warm like summer sun rays and tastes like honey and I carry it in the palm of my hands. Hope surrounds me but only in my dreams, only when I am asleep does hope come to me.

Lung Capacity

"I don't know how to express myself"

But you do. You express yourself in the way you stand while doing dishes. In the way you fold your towels and the candle you pick out for that week. You express yourself in the way you walk and run, in the laugh that bubbles out of you at a joke and in the gentleness you carry at your fingertips when you touch something you are in awe of. You express yourself when you choose to take a bath instead of a shower and add bubbles to feel closer to your inner child. When you add milk and sugar into your coffee or decide to drink only water for a day. You don't have to use words to express yourself because you do it in the way you pick up an orange to examine it before placing it into your basket and how you stir your tea. In the way you stretch in the mornings and in the way you brush your teeth. You express yourself completely, so loudly, during the mundane hours of every day.

Lung Capacity

When I die and my body begins to rot, who will sit with me in the mortuary and tell me stories of a faraway land they hope my soul has gone to? Who will hold my cold hand and tell me I am safe in this unknown place even when the lights are shut off and they're told it's time to go? Who is going to visit me when I'm planted into the earth like a seed and it's time for people to start forgetting me?

Lung Capacity

The morning after I killed myself I remembered how God took my face in his hands and screamed, *"Do you not see the beauty I have created for you?"* and I confessed to him that the sickness that infects my brain has muted the colors of life.

The morning after I killed myself I placed my bare feet on my hardwood floors and listened to the patterning of my steps echoing down the hall. My brother was asleep on the couch — TV remote in his hand and my mom was cooking breakfast and humming a tune from my childhood. I heard the shower running and knew my sister would use most of my brand-new shampoo and probably steal a sweater from my closet and look better in it than I do.

The morning after I killed myself a blue jay sat on my windowsill and made faces at me. He sang me a song and reminded me that everything in nature is a form of art. My cat slept on the pillow, and the dog silently asked to climb onto the bed with a wagging tail and the look of *please*. I watched the wind chime sway in the wind and clink together as I inhaled the scent of freshly mowed grass and summer morning rain.

The morning after I killed myself, life came to my funeral and kissed my purple lips. *"live"* she whispered in my ear and my lungs filled with fresh air and the promise of a better life.

Mae Setrova

Lung Capacity

When I die, I want to be turned to ash so everyone I've ever loved can have pieces of me. But I don't want to be placed in an urn on top of mantles or dressers next to photos or inside of silver necklace lockets.

I want to be planted with the seeds in flower beds so I can bloom every spring in the form of different flowers and they can hold me again.
I want them to place me in the earth with young tree roots before they're planted and use my ashes as part of a new tattoo so that I am always there.
And when it's all over, I want them to throw what's left of me into the ocean — when the sun is rising and the water is calm so they will never have to fear forgetting me because they'll remember who I was and the life I lived when the ocean water runs over their toes.

I will live on forever in these moments, within these places. I will never be completely gone because I will be everywhere and *that* will be my eternity.

Lung Capacity

You're going to wake up one day and feel excited to be alive. You're going to discover a new show one day, and it's going to become your favorite and you'll rewatch it every couple of months with that nostalgic feeling in your chest. You're going to meet new people, and they're going to feel like they're a part of your soul — a reason for your existence and you're going to think *"How did I ever live without these people?"* One day, you're going to wake up and the world will still be spinning and you'll no longer be angry at it for moving on. You will feel every breath your lungs take and feel euphoric during each exhale. One day, you'll find your way back to yourself and meet who you are meant to be, and it will be better than you ever imagined.

Lung Capacity

Spring is here and I will spend the coming months brushing the bruises winter left from my hair. I will say goodbye to yesterday and forget my heartbreaks in a jar of strawberry moonshine on a warm July night and pluck fresh blackberries through the fence in my front yard. The birds will sing, and in their song I will feel my lungs thaw and take my first real breath since August and I'll rid of the dust collecting on my unused heart.

Spring has come again and taken my hand, pulling me towards the river's edge and reminding me that winter is long but not forever, and I will be reborn with the wildflowers every year.

Lung Capacity

What if you never leave this small town, and you go to a college nearby where you meet a boy with eyes the color of soil and you graduate together, then move into a shoe box of an apartment where you adopt a kitten and your life together begins right there in unfurnished space.

But what if you do leave that small town, and you decide to study abroad and you see the world, and eat foods you've never heard of and leave pieces of your heart in every city you step foot in. You fall in love — not with a boy but the wonder of life and when you graduate you pack up your life into a handful of boxes and go to an unknown place full of people you don't know and you turn it into a home.

What then?
What if you dared to dream that big?

Lung Capacity

The trees are dying
but this is still their most
beautiful state.

October reminds us
that even the end of something great
can be a beautiful thing.

Lung Capacity

One day I will die, and I won't be there to see my funeral or comfort the ones I love most when the loss of me takes over their lives. I won't be there to gently wipe away their tears when the memory of me appears like a ghost in their passenger seats because a song I used to love begins to fill the car and they have to pull over to mourn their loss for the third time that day. People will grieve my death, they will mourn my life and all of its loss because even though I feel insignificant, I know I am anything but in the lives intertwined with my own. Those I love will mourn my absence so hard some days that their lungs will fail to give them any air but they will be okay. The wounds my death will cause will heal with time. They will fade into healed scars that don't hurt to touch the way they did the first few months without me and I will no longer be a subject too painful to talk about.

This is just a brief pause until I see you again.

Mae Setrova

Lung Capacity

For the souls that ache

sisterhood, girlhood, growing up.

Lung Capacity

My sister thinks I can't stand to be around her because I never look directly at her when she speaks but the truth is it hurts too much. I love her, I would give my life to buy her more time on earth but I envy her, of all the things she never had to grow up knowing or being aware of. We were raised by the same people in the same house and yet our childhoods were entirely separate. She got to keep the innocence of a child while I lost mine protecting hers and I am happy she didn't have to go through the same but I am still angry that I wasn't protected, too.

Lung Capacity

"Do you think we're sisters in every universe?"
I think that no matter what is taking place in other universes, we are always something to each other.

There's probably a world out there where you're my mother, and I'm sitting between your legs on a school night while you braid my wet hair before bed as we sing along to the entire Tangled soundtrack.

And there's probably another where you're my best friend, and we are sitting on my bed telling each other about boys that only give us crumbs for 'love' but for teenage girls that have never experienced anything different, it's enough.

Maybe we meet at a grocery store, in a world where I'm the short one and can't reach a box of captain crunch so you reach up and grab it for me, and we make conversation for an hour until we part ways and become the type of strangers you always remember.

Whatever it is, no matter what is taking place in these universes, we are always something to each other. *You could never be nothing to me.*

Lung Capacity

We are 16 and 19, and in an attempt to revisit our childhood one last time before we let it go, we sneak into our mother's room and lay her dresses across her bed and try on every pair of shoes we find hiding under piles of dust in her closet. We rummage through her makeup box, applying dark eyeshadows and red lipsticks to each other's faces like blank canvases and giggle like the little girls we once were.

It's nearly 1 am. The lighting is dim but our spirits are bright as we take photos of our ridiculous state. The little girls that are still within us are happy and for a few hours, we don't pay attention to the way our mother's clothes fit us just fine now.

Lung Capacity

The morning before my 10th birthday I cried to my mother about how I didn't want to grow another year older. I wasn't ready to grow up and take another step closer to the end of my childlike innocence and the time, turning 10 felt like the end of it.

"Let me wake up tomorrow morning 7 years old again" I whispered into my birthday candles as their little flames went out and the room echoed with applause and cheers.

They celebrated another year I gained while I mourned the ones I had already lost.

Lung Capacity

I long for more childlike years
and life-changing moments
built out of simplicity
knowing they will not come.

Lung Capacity

The corners of the houses you once knew so well have become foreign places to you. You no longer know where the extra bath towels are stored or which floorboards creak when stepped on. The alarms go off at different hours than before and new people have moved into the house down the street where you used to play. There was once a time you could have walked through this house blindfolded but now you find yourself running into coffee tables and tripping over rugs that weren't always there.

The houses that were once your entire childhood have become only drywall and pieces of furniture.

Lung Capacity

I sometimes wonder if I will still care this deeply about the way I look when I am an old woman looking back on photographs taken during my youth.

I worry that I won't escape this sort of disappointment at the sight of myself even when my hair fades of color and wrinkles begin to show on every inch of my face. I worry I'll stand in front of a mirror fixated on every wrinkle and imperfect laugh line I see until I am driven mad with trying to find a way to look prettier or younger.

Will I always carry insecurity around with me like it is a tube of my favorite mascara or will I learn to drop its hand?

Lung Capacity

Lung Capacity

End Note

Thank you from the bottom of my heart for reading my book. It's generic and you will find this in every poet's book somewhere along the lines but I have been dreaming of this since I was a child, so to say I have a published book is the most surreal experience in the world to me. I never expected this to happen when I first started sharing my poems on the internet as a way to cope with my heartache and I still can't wrap my head around the opportunities it has given me. I will never be able to thank everyone who supported me nearly enough, or ever repay the kindness.

Lung Capacity

Lung Capacity

About Author

Mae Setrova is a poet from West Virginia who keeps her identity hidden behind the pen name, Setrova. Her love for poetry was discovered when she read a Charles Bukowski poem written in marker on the side of a bathroom stall when she was eight years old and her love for the art form has only grown from there. Mae first started sharing her poetry on TikTok over the summer of 2021 where her first post to the platform then went viral. She has since deleted the poem and refuses to let it see the light of day ever again.

Made in United States
Orlando, FL
27 October 2024